D1542428

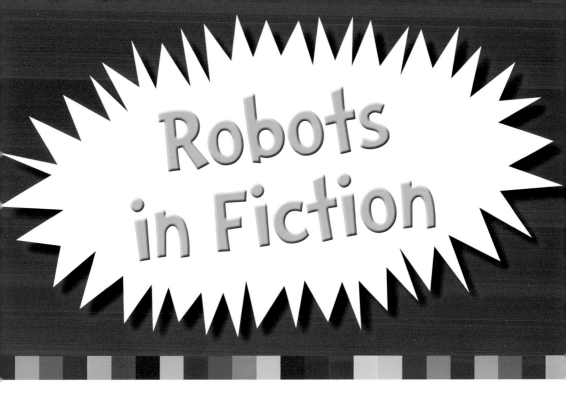

Robots in Fiction

BY NADIA HIGGINS

AMICUS HIGH INTEREST • AMICUS INK

Amicus High Interest and Amicus Ink are imprints of Amicus
P.O. Box 1329, Mankato, MN 56002
www.amicuspublishing.us

Library of Congress Cataloging-in-Publication Data
Names: Higgins, Nadia, author.
Title: Robots in fiction / by Nadia Higgins.
Description: Mankato, Minnesota : Amicus Ink, 2018. | Series:
  Robotics in our world | Includes index.
Identifiers: LCCN 2016041969 (print) | LCCN 2016043744
  (ebook) | ISBN 9781681511467 (library binding) | ISBN
  9781681521770 (pbk.) | ISBN 9781681512365 (ebook)
  | ISBN 9781681512365 (pdf)
Subjects: LCSH: Robots–Juvenile literature. | Robots in
  literature–Juvenile literature. | Robots in motion pictures–
  Juvenile literature.
Classification: LCC TJ211.2 .H47 2018 (print) | LCC TJ211.2
  (ebook) | DDC 809/.9336–dc23
LC record available at https://lccn.loc.gov/2016041969

Editor: Wendy Dieker
Series Designer: Kathleen Petelinsek
Book Designer: Tracy Myers
Photo Researcher: Holly Young

Photo Credits: Sarunyu L/Shutterstock.com cover; Walt Disney
Pictures/Pixar Animation Studios/Ronald Grant Archive/Mary
Evans 5, 22-23; Columbia/Buena Vista/Ronald Grant Archive/
Mary Evans 6; Imagno/Hulton Archive/Getty 9; Rex Features/
Snap Stills/REX/Shutterstock 10; Collection Christophel/Alamy
Stock Photo 13, 26; Moviestore Collection Ltd/Alamy Stock
Photo 14-15; AF archive/Alamy Stock Photo 17, 18, 28-29;
Photos 12/Alamy Stock Photo 21; Pictorial Press Ltd/Alamy
Stock Photo 25

Printed in the United States of America

HC 10 9 8 7 6 5 4 3 2 1
PB 10 9 8 7 6 5 4 3 2 1

Table of Contents

Amazing Powers　　　　4

The Original Robots　　8

Evil Robots　　　　　15

Lovable Robots　　　　20

What If?　　　　　　28

Glossary　　　　　30

Read More　　　　　31

Websites　　　　　31

Index　　　　　　32

Amazing Powers

Robots in fiction live in made-up stories. But that does not mean the stories are totally untrue. Writers can look at the amazing powers of real-life robots. In a factory, a robot arm can lift a car. A person programs and controls that robot. But what if robots didn't need people? What if they could walk out of the factory? A fiction writer shows what *might* happen.

EVE is a robot in the movie *WALL-E.* In the story, she looks for plants.

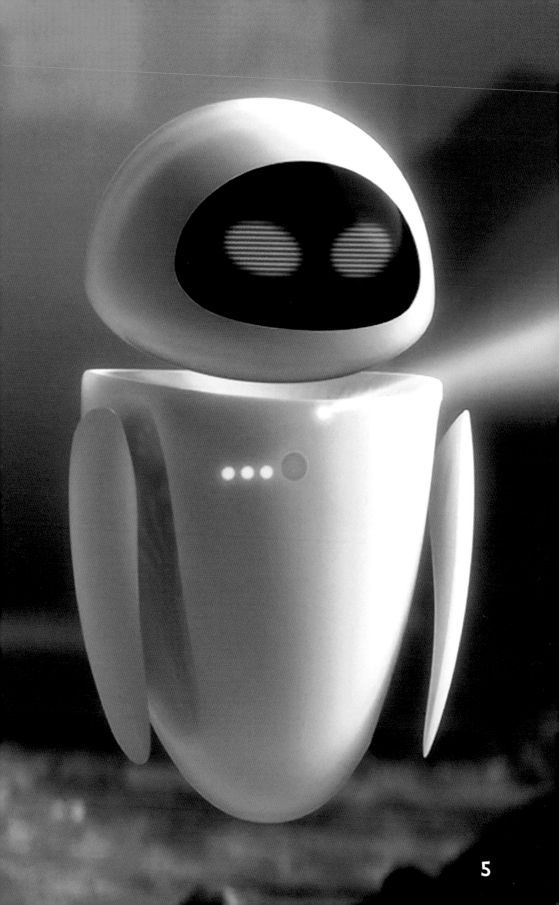

Bicentennial Man is a story about a robot who wants to be a real man.

Robots in stories can be fast and strong. They can sometimes come back to life. Their super brains can solve problems in a microsecond. Fictional robots can be monsters or friends. Sometimes they are funny. Some seem to have feelings. What is your favorite kind of robot story?

The Original Robots

Robots in fiction go back hundreds of years. Talos is a fighter in Greek **myths**. His metal body heats up. He kills enemies with a sizzling hug.

Fast forward to 1921. Karel Capek's play *R.U.R.* came out. In this story, artificial humans take over the world. Capek called them *roboti*. It came from his language, called Czech. The word robot was born.

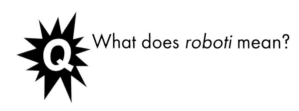 What does *roboti* mean?

**A scene from the play *R.U.R.*
shows new robots in a factory.**

It comes from a word that means "slave work."
Robots in Capek's play were built to be slaves

Many of Asimov's stories have been made into movies. This scene is from *I, Robot*.

In 1942, Isaac Asimov invented the Three Laws of Robotics. They lay out how humans and robots should get along. A robot may not harm humans. A robot must obey humans. Finally, it must protect its own life. Other writers began to play around with the rules. What if a robot harms the planet? What about animals? The laws sparked many **science fiction** stories. People like to imagine what robots could do.

Soon robots became popular in movies, too. In 1977, *Star Wars* brought us R2-D2 and C-3PO. These guys were a new kind of robot. They were brave and loyal. And they were funny. R2-D2 can fix anything. C-3PO is such a smooth talker. Together, they come to the rescue time and again.

R2-D2 (left) and C-3PO (right) are two famous fictional robots. They appear in *Star Wars* stories.

Evil Robots

Megatron started as a toy in 1984. Soon, he was a character in a cartoon and a series of movies. But this Transformer is anything but playful. He rules an evil race of robots. His mission? Kill and destroy. Megatron's body can change into weapons. One blast from his arm can wipe out a city block.

Megatron appears in many movies, TV shows, and comic books. He is a robot **villain**.

Dr. Octopus is a **mad scientist**. He built the robotic arms that grow from his back. The arms make him a match for Spider-Man. Is Dr. Octopus robot or human? Both. He is a **cyborg**. He controls the arms by thinking. The arms come off, too. He sends them away to do his evil plans.

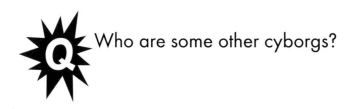
Who are some other cyborgs?

Dr. Octopus's robotic arms are part of stories about Spider-Man.

 Darth Vader and Iron Man, for starters. They use their brain power to control robotic body parts.

The Borg is a **swarm** of cyborgs from the *Star Trek* TV show and movies. Borgs want just one thing—your brain. They attack with needles that shoot from their hands. Tiny machines go into a **victim**'s blood. His personality is erased. His thoughts are no longer his own. He is now part of the Borg.

People captured by the Borg often have robotic parts added to their bodies.

Lovable Robots

While some robots spread evil, others save the day. BB-8 from *Star Wars* is like R2-D2's little brother. This adorable guy has one very important job. He must deliver a map that leads to Luke Skywalker. Poor BB-8. All the bad guys are after him. But he just keeps on rolling.

In the movie, was BB-8 drawn by computers?

The rolling robot BB-8 shows that robots in stories can be friendly.

 No. BB-8 was a real **prop**. He moved on set with the actors.

WALL-E rolls around piles of trash. He is looking for things to collect. Way in the future, Earth has been destroyed. WALL-E thinks he is the last robot on Earth. Then EVE shows up. A robot love story begins. They have quite a space adventure, too. These two robots must save Earth before it is too late.

WALL-E travels to space in this story about the future.

Baymax from *Big Hero 6* looks like a pool toy. This puffy robot has one main job. He protects Hiro, his teenage master. Then a bad guy shows up. Hiro programs Baymax to become a superhero. In his armor, Baymax becomes a fierce fighter. He can catch falling buildings. He can fly across space. But he always stays gentle inside.

Why are robots usually boys?

Baymax from *Big Hero 6* wears red and blue armor to fight. But he's a sweet robot.

 People often think of robots as boy stuff. But that old idea is changing. Girls like robots, too!

Athena from the movie *Tomorrowland* was built to do a job. Athena looks exactly like a human, but she is a robot with super powers and x-ray vision. She was sent to Earth to find smart people. She invites these people to Tomorrowland, a futuristic place where robots and people live and work. She finds a way to help save Earth.

When people in Tomorrowland want to destroy Earth, Athena works to save the planet.

What If?

Robots in fiction have amazing powers. Iron Man's robotic armor makes him super strong. Could a robot help a person like that in real life? Maybe! In real life, robotic suits are helping people. **Exoskeletons** give strength to people who cannot walk. What if you could choose? What robot power would you make real?

Tony Stark fixes his robotic suit in *Iron Man.* How can robots help us in real life?

Glossary

cyborg A creature that is part robot, part human.

exoskeleton Robotic parts that fit on a person's body, such as over the legs; exoskeletons give strength and help people walk.

mad scientist A brilliant scientist who is also evil.

myth A kind of story that was told by people long ago.

prop An item used on the set of a play or movie.

science fiction A kind of story that imagines life in the future or on another planet.

swarm A group of creatures that all work together.

victim Someone who is the target of evil.

villain An evil character in a work of fiction.

Read More

Bell, Cece. *Rabbit and Robot: The Sleepover.* Somerville, Mass.: Candlewick Press, 2012.

DiPucchio, Kelly. *Clink.* New York: Balzer & Bray, 2011.

Dyckman, Ame. *Boy + Bot.* New York: Alfred A. Knopf, 2012.

Websites

Common Sense Media: Best Robot Movies
https://www.commonsensemedia.org/lists/best-robot-movies

Goodreads: Robots for Kids
https://www.goodreads.com/list/show/34858.Robots_For_Kids

R2-D2 Sounds
http://www.soundboard.com/sb/R2D2_R2_D2_sounds

Index

Asimov, Isaac 11

Athena 27

Baymax 24

BB-8 20, 21

Big Hero 6 24

Borg 19

C-3PO 12

Capek, Karel 8

cyborgs 16, 17, 19

Darth Vader 17

Dr. Octopus 16

factory robots 4

Greek myths 8

Iron Man 17, 28

Megatron 15

R.U.R. 8, 9

R2-D2 12, 20

Star Trek 19

Star Wars 12, 20, 21

Talos 8

Three Laws of Robotics
  11

Tomorrowland 27

Transformers 15

WALL-E 23

About the Author

Nadia Higgins is the author of more than 100 books for children and young adults. She has written about everything from ants to zombies, with many science and technology topics in between. Higgins lives in Minneapolis, Minnesota, with her human family, pet lizard, and robotic dog.